MATTHEW PERRY BIOGRAPHY

From Laughter to Legacy – A Journey Worth Remembering.

Harry A. Wilson

COPYRIGHT NOTICE

TABLE OF CONTENT

INTRODUCTION TO MATTHEW PERRY

Matthew Perry, born on August 19, 1969, in Williamstown, Massachusetts, is a name synonymous with entertainment, laughter, and heart-warming moments on the silver screen. He is an actor, writer, and producer who has left an indelible mark on the world of film and television. In this biography, we delve into the life of a man whose journey has been marked by both triumph and tribulation.

From the outset, it's evident that Matthew Perry's story is one of perseverance, resilience, and the pursuit of excellence. As we explore his life, we will come to understand the actor beyond the characters he portrayed on screen. We will look beyond the witty and sarcastic Chandler Bing from the iconic television series "Friends" or the lovable Oscar Madison from the modern adaptation of "The Odd Couple."

This biography seeks to capture the essence of Matthew Perry, the man behind the roles, and his profound impact on the world of entertainment. It's a tale of a young boy with a dream, a dream that evolved into a remarkable career in Hollywood.

Throughout these pages, we will uncover the layers of Matthew Perry's life. We'll discuss his early years and family background, understanding the influences that shaped him into the actor and individual he became. We will explore his journey into the world of acting, from his humble beginnings to his rise to stardom, and the challenges he faced along the way.

But this biography is not just about his professional achievements; it's a deep dive into his personal life, his struggles, and his triumphs. We will discuss his battles with addiction and the courage it took to overcome them. We will explore his resurgence in Hollywood and his multifaceted talents, including his forays into writing, producing, and his dedication to philanthropy and social activism.

Matthew Perry's story is not just one of personal success; it's also a tale of giving back. His advocacy for mental health and his work in raising awareness about this critical issue have had a profound impact beyond the entertainment industry. We will examine his role as a voice in mental health advocacy and the legacy he is leaving in this field.

As we progress through this biography, we will reflect on Matthew Perry's influence on pop culture, particularly through his role in "Friends" and the highly anticipated "Friends Reunion." We'll also take a closer look at unexplored aspects of his life and share personal insights and anecdotes from those who have known him.

Ultimately, this biography aims to unveil the enigma that is Matthew Perry, shedding light on the man who has brought joy to millions through his work. Beyond the biography, we will discuss his lasting impact on the entertainment industry and the lessons we can learn from his journey.

Join us on this remarkable journey through the life of Matthew Perry, a man whose career has made us laugh, cry, and think. This is the story of a beloved actor, writer, and philanthropist, and the mark he has left on the world.

HISTORICAL CONTEXT OF MATTHEW PERRY

To fully appreciate the life and career of Matthew Perry, it's essential to understand the historical context in which he was born and came of age. The era in which an individual grows up often shapes their values, aspirations, and opportunities. Matthew Perry, born on August 19, 1969, in Williamstown, Massachusetts, was no exception. Let's explore the historical backdrop against which his journey unfolded.

The Late 20th Century America:

Matthew Perry's formative years took place during the late 20th century, a period marked by significant social, political, and cultural changes. This was the era of the Cold War, with tensions between the United States and the Soviet Union looming large. The world was gripped by the fear of nuclear conflict, and it heavily influenced the global geopolitical landscape.

Rise of Television:

The 1980s and 1990s were a golden age of television. This era witnessed the proliferation of cable television and the emergence of iconic shows that would go on to become cultural touchstones. Matthew Perry's entry into the entertainment world as an actor coincided with this television boom.

The Tech Revolution:

The late 20th century also saw the advent of the personal computer and the internet, innovations that would eventually reshape the way we live, work, and communicate. While Matthew Perry is best known for his work in television and film, these technological advancements would play a crucial role in the evolution of the entertainment industry.

Pop Culture and Music:

This period was defined by the rise of pop culture icons and influential music. It was the era of rock 'n' roll, hip-hop, and the birth of the MTV generation. Music and pop culture played an integral role in shaping the tastes and preferences of a generation, including young Matthew Perry.

Social and Political Changes:

The late 20th century was marked by significant social and political changes. It witnessed the end of apartheid in South Africa, the fall of the Berlin Wall, and the dissolution of the Soviet Union. In the United States, there were movements for civil rights and advancements in LGBTQ+ rights, all of which would contribute to a changing social landscape.

The Entertainment Industry:

Hollywood and the entertainment industry experienced transformative changes during this period. The 1990s, in particular, saw a surge in independent filmmaking and the emergence of new talent. Matthew Perry's journey into acting and his subsequent success in the entertainment industry were influenced by the trends and developments of this era.

Globalization:

The late 20th century marked the beginnings of increased globalization. The world was becoming more interconnected, and cultural exchange was on the rise. This globalization had a significant impact on the entertainment industry, expanding the reach and influence of Hollywood.

Understanding the historical context in which Matthew Perry's life and career unfolded provides us with valuable insights into the influences and opportunities that shaped him. As we delve deeper into his biography, we will see how these historical factors played a role in his journey from a small-town boy to a celebrated actor and influential figure in the entertainment world.

CHAPTER ONE

EARLY LIFE AND FAMILY OF MATTHEW PERRY

Matthew Perry's journey from a small town in Massachusetts to becoming a beloved figure in the world of entertainment is a testament to his resilience and determination. Understanding his early life and the influence of his family on his upbringing is crucial to appreciating the man behind the iconic roles he portrayed on screen.

1. A Small-Town Beginning:

Matthew Langford Perry was born on August 19, 1969, in Williamstown, Massachusetts. This picturesque New England town served as the backdrop for his formative years. It's in this small town that he developed the foundation for his future success.

2. A Family of Actors:

The apple doesn't fall far from the tree, and in Matthew Perry's case, his family had a significant influence on his choice of career. His father, John Bennett Perry, was an actor and former model, while his mother, Suzanne Morrison, was a Canadian journalist and press secretary to the Canadian Prime Minister Pierre Trudeau. Matthew's stepfather, Keith Morrison, is a well-known television journalist.

3. The Impact of Divorce:

Matthew's parents divorced when he was still a child, which undoubtedly had an impact on his early life. This experience, while challenging, may have contributed to the depth and complexity he brought to his later roles, particularly in portraying characters dealing with personal struggles.

4. Education and Early Interests:

Matthew attended Ashbury College, a prestigious private school in Ottawa, Canada. He was a bright student but struggled with dyslexia, a learning disability that would later become a part of his personal narrative. Despite his challenges, he developed a love for acting and was involved in school productions, which sparked his interest in the craft.

5. Moving to Hollywood:

Following his high school graduation, Perry decided to follow in his father's footsteps and pursue a career in acting. He moved to Hollywood, where he began his journey as an actor. It was a bold move for a young man from a small town, but it marked the beginning of a remarkable career.

6. Family Support:

The support and encouragement of his family were instrumental in Matthew's pursuit of an acting career. Their experiences in the entertainment industry likely provided valuable insights and guidance as he navigated the complex and competitive world of Hollywood.

7. Early Struggles:

Matthew Perry's path to success was not without its challenges. Like many aspiring actors, he faced auditions, rejections, and the uncertainty that comes with pursuing a career in the entertainment industry. His early years in Hollywood were marked by perseverance and determination.

8. The Influence of Family Values:

Despite the glamorous world of Hollywood, Matthew Perry has often emphasized the importance of family values and groundedness. His upbringing in a supportive and close-knit family likely played a role in shaping his down-to-earth and relatable persona, which endeared him to audiences.

9. Turning Personal Experiences into Art:

Throughout his career, Perry drew on his personal experiences and family influences to add depth and authenticity to the characters he portrayed. His ability to infuse his roles with genuine emotion and humour made him a standout talent in the industry.

Understanding Matthew Perry's childhood and family background will provide insight into the origins of his determination, talent, and the personal struggles he would later face.

These early experiences laid the foundation for his remarkable journey in the world of entertainment which we will explore in more detail as we continue to delve deeper into his biography.

CHAPTER TWO

THE ROAD TO STARDOM: MATTHEW PERRY'S JOURNEY

Matthew Perry's road to stardom was a remarkable and arduous journey marked by dedication, passion, and numerous challenges. From his early aspirations to his breakthrough role on the small screen, every step he took brought him closer to becoming one of the most recognizable actors in the world.

1. Early Aspirations:

Matthew's dream of becoming an actor began to take shape during his formative years. His love for the craft was kindled through school plays and the influence of his father, John Bennett Perry, who was an actor. These early experiences ignited a passion that would drive him to pursue his dreams.

2. The Move to Hollywood:

At the age of 18, Matthew took a significant step by moving to Hollywood, the epicentre of the entertainment industry. This move was a pivotal moment in his journey, as it marked the beginning of his pursuit of an acting career.

3. Initial Struggles:

Like many aspiring actors, Matthew Perry faced the inevitable struggles of auditions, rejections, and the uncertainty of making a living in Hollywood. These early years tested his determination and commitment to his craft.

4. Breakthrough Roles:

Matthew's dedication paid off when he secured his first television roles, including appearances in series like "Charles in

Charge" and "Sydney." However, it was his role as Chazz Russell in the hit series "Second Chance" that put him on the map and garnered attention for his comedic talent.

5. "Friends" and the Role of Chandler Bing:

The turning point in Matthew Perry's career came when he auditioned for the role of Chandler Bing on the iconic television series "Friends." The chemistry between the ensemble cast was electric, and the show quickly became a cultural phenomenon.

Matthew's portrayal of Chandler, the lovable, sarcastic, and witty character, earned him critical acclaim and a massive fan following. "Friends" was a game-changer for Perry, catapulting him to stardom and making him a household name.

6. Impact and Legacy:

"Friends" went on to become one of the most successful and enduring sitcoms in television history. Matthew Perry's role in the show not only brought him fame but also cemented his status as a comedic genius. His catchphrases and comedic timing are still beloved by fans worldwide.

7. Film Success:

Matthew Perry's success extended beyond the small screen. He ventured into the world of film, with roles in movies like "Fools Rush In," "The Whole Nine Yards," and "The Whole Ten Yards." These films showcased his versatility as an actor and solidified his position in the industry.

8. Challenges Along the Way:

While the world saw Matthew Perry as a talented actor, he faced personal challenges, including battles with addiction. His struggles with substance abuse and his journey to recovery added a layer of complexity to his life and career.

9. Continued Relevance:

Matthew Perry's stardom was not confined to the '90s. He continued to be a relevant figure in the entertainment industry, taking on various roles in television, film, and stage productions.

10. Reflection on Success:

Matthew Perry's journey to stardom is a testament to his talent, resilience, and the unwavering support of his fans. Throughout his career, he remained humble and appreciative of the opportunities he received.

Matthew Perry's path to stardom has been a remarkable adventure, helping him rise from a young actor with dreams to become a globally recognized star.

His journey, full of ups and downs, is a testament to the enduring power of determination and talent in the entertainment world.

CHAPTER THREE

ICONIC ROLES IN FILM AND TELEVISION: MATTHEW PERRY'S ACTING ODYSSEY

Matthew Perry's journey through the world of film and television is punctuated by an array of iconic roles that have left an indelible mark on the industry and the hearts of viewers. His remarkable talent, impeccable comedic timing, and versatility as an actor have made him a beloved figure on both the big and small screens. Let's delve into some of his most memorable roles.

1. Chandler Bing in "Friends" (1994-2004):

Undoubtedly, the role that defines Matthew Perry's career is Chandler Bing on the iconic television series "Friends."

Chandler's sarcastic wit and endearing quirks made him one of the standout characters on the show. Perry's portrayal of Chandler earned him critical acclaim and a dedicated fan base. His catchphrases, such as "Could I BE any more...," and his unique comedic style continue to be celebrated by fans around the world.

2. Chazz Russell in "Second Chance" (1987):

Early in his career, Perry gained attention for his role as Chazz Russell in the series "Second Chance." This marked one of his first notable roles and hinted at his comedic prowess.

3. Oscar Novak in "Fools Rush In" (1997):

In this romantic comedy, Perry starred alongside Salma Hayek, playing the role of Oscar Novak, an uptight architect. The film showcased his ability to deliver both humour and heartfelt moments.

4. Nicholas "Oz" Oseransky in "The Whole Nine Yards" (2000):

Perry's role as Nicholas "Oz" Oseransky, a meek dentist, in "The Whole Nine Yards" marked a departure from his Chandler Bing persona. The film was a commercial success and demonstrated his versatility as an actor.

5. Ray "Ray" Jones in "The Whole Ten Yards" (2004):

Perry reprised his role as Oz in the sequel "The Whole Ten Yards," proving his comedic talents could sustain a franchise.

6. Ryan King in "Go On" (2012-2013):

After "Friends," Perry returned to television as Ryan King, a sports talk radio host, in the series "Go On." The show showcased his ability to tackle both comedy and drama, as his character navigated the complexities of grief and healing.

7. Walter in "The End of Longing" (2016):

Perry made his playwriting debut with "The End of Longing" and also starred in it. The play explored themes of addiction and relationships, and his performance received critical acclaim.

8. Ron Clark in "The Ron Clark Story" (2006):

Perry portrayed the real-life educator Ron Clark in this television film. His portrayal of Clark, a dedicated teacher who makes a difference in the lives of his students, showcased his ability to take on more dramatic roles.

9. Ted Kennedy in "The Kennedys: After Camelot" (2017):

Perry took on the challenging role of Ted Kennedy in the miniseries "The Kennedys:

After Camelot." The series explored the post-Camelot years of the Kennedy family, and his performance was met with praise.

Matthew Perry's ability to easily transition from comedy to drama, his talent for delivering memorable lines, and his dedication to his craft have solidified his status as an iconic figure in the world of entertainment.

His roles are not only entertaining but also help audiences better understand the complexities of human relationships and emotions.

Perry's contributions to film and television continue to be celebrated, ensuring that his legacy as an actor will live on for generations to come.

CHAPTER FOUR

BEHIND THE SCENES: MATTHEW PERRY'S PERSONAL LIFE

While Matthew Perry is best known for his on-screen roles, his personal life has been a complex and, at times, challenging journey. Understanding the man behind the characters he portrays is essential to appreciating his resilience, his triumphs, and his commitment to making a difference in the world.

1. Battles with Addiction:

One of the most significant aspects of Matthew Perry's personal life has been his well-documented struggles with addiction. His battle with substance abuse began during the early days of "Friends" and continued for years. His openness about these challenges has allowed him to connect with those facing similar issues and has inspired many on the path to recovery.

2. Road to Recovery:

Perry's journey to recovery has been an ongoing process. He has openly shared his experiences in rehabilitation and the ongoing commitment to maintaining sobriety. His efforts to help others struggling with addiction have been a testament to his personal growth and resilience.

3. Personal Relationships:

Throughout his life, Matthew Perry's personal relationships have been the subject of media scrutiny. His romantic involvements, friendships, and the dynamics of his personal life have been a topic of interest for fans and tabloids alike.

4. Philanthropic Ventures:

Beyond the glitz and glamour of Hollywood, Perry's personal life has been characterized by a strong sense of giving back. He has been actively involved in philanthropic endeavours, particularly those related to drug addiction and recovery. His commitment to raising awareness about the challenges of addiction has made a significant impact on the lives of many.

5. Mental Health Advocacy:

Perry has used his personal experiences to become a vocal advocate for mental health awareness. His advocacy and involvement in organizations dedicated to mental health have made him a recognized figure in this critical area. By sharing his own struggles, he has helped destigmatize conversations around mental health.

6. Creative Pursuits:

Matthew Perry's personal life also includes his creative pursuits beyond acting. He ventured into writing, and his play, "The End of Longing," explored themes of addiction and relationships. This demonstrated his multifaceted talents and his desire to engage in projects that reflect his personal interests and passions.

7. A Private Individual:

While Perry has been open about certain aspects of his personal life, he remains a relatively private individual. His ability to balance his public persona with a desire for personal privacy has added to his mystique and enigma.

8. Health Struggles:

In addition to his battles with addiction, Perry has faced various health challenges, including surgeries related to a gastrointestinal perforation. His candidness about these health issues has prompted important discussions around health and well-being.

9. Pursuit of Happiness:

Matthew Perry's personal life journey can be summarized as a quest for happiness, fulfilment, and personal growth. His dedication to maintaining his sobriety, his philanthropic work, and his creative pursuits all reflect his determination to lead a meaningful and purposeful life.

Getting a behind-the-scenes look at Matthew Perry's personal life is a testament to his resilience and depth of character.

His transparency about his efforts and commitment to making a positive impact endeared him to his fans and made him a role model for those facing similar challenges.

Perry's journey, both in the spotlight and behind the scenes, is a testament to people's ability to grow, change, and make a difference in their lives.

BATTLES WITH ADDICTION: MATTHEW PERRY'S PERSONAL STRUGGLES

Matthew Perry's battles with addiction are a significant and widely known aspect of his life story. His journey through addiction and recovery has been marked by both personal challenges and the resilience to overcome them. This section delves into the harrowing but ultimately inspiring saga of his struggles with addiction.

1. Early Experiences:

Matthew Perry's introduction to substance abuse occurred during his early years in Hollywood. The pressures of the entertainment industry, coupled with a desire to fit in and escape from stress, led to his initial experimentation with drugs and alcohol.

2. The Height of "Friends":

Perry's addiction struggles paralleled the monumental success of "Friends," which became a cultural phenomenon in the 1990s. The pressures and demands of fame intensified during this time, exacerbating his substance abuse.

3. Professional and Personal Consequences:

Perry's addiction took a toll on his personal life and his work. It led to deteriorating relationships, missed opportunities, and health issues. Despite the success of

"Friends," the personal battles he fought off-screen were a stark contrast to the laughter he brought to millions on-screen.

4. Multiple Rehab Stints:

Over the years, Perry sought treatment through multiple rehabilitation programs in an effort to combat his addiction. These stints in rehab were reflective of his acknowledgment of the need for help and his commitment to recovery.

5. Relapses and Setbacks:

Recovery from addiction is often marked by relapses and setbacks, and Perry's journey was no exception. He candidly shared that he struggled with relapses during his path to sobriety.

6. A Turning Point:

The turning point in Perry's life came when he realized the need for profound change. He recognized the destructive nature of addiction and made a conscious decision to prioritize recovery.

7. Commitment to Sobriety:

Matthew Perry's commitment to sobriety is a testament to his strength of character. He has openly discussed how sobriety has allowed him to take control of his life and achieve personal and professional success.

8. Using His Experience for Good:

Perry has turned his personal struggles into a force for good. His candidness about addiction has inspired others to seek help and has contributed to the broader conversation on addiction and recovery.

9. Philanthropic Efforts:

Perry's journey through addiction led him to become a vocal advocate for those facing similar challenges. He has been actively involved in philanthropic efforts related to drug addiction and recovery, including his work with the Perry House, a sober living facility.

10. Lessons Learned:

Matthew Perry's battles with addiction have provided valuable lessons not only for him but for those who have followed his story. He has emphasized the importance of seeking help, finding a supportive community, and never giving up on the path to recovery.

11. An Ongoing Journey:

Perry's recovery journey is ongoing. He continues to prioritize his health and sobriety, using his experiences to guide others who may be struggling.

Matthew Perry's battle with addiction is a powerful and relevant aspect of his life story.

His transparency about his struggles and his commitment to recovery have made him an inspiration to many.

Her story proves that even in the darkest of times, there is hope and potential for transformation.

Perry's personal victory over addiction reminds us that with determination and support, even the most difficult obstacles can be overcome.

THE ROAD TO RECOVERY: MATTHEW PERRY'S INSPIRING JOURNEY

Matthew Perry's path to recovery from addiction is a story of resilience, self-discovery, and the unwavering determination to overcome one of the most challenging aspects of his life. His journey serves as a testament to the human spirit's capacity for growth and transformation. In this section, we explore his road to recovery in detail.

1. **Acknowledgment and Acceptance:**

Recovery often begins with acknowledging the problem and accepting the need for change. For Matthew Perry, this was a pivotal moment. He recognized that his addiction had taken control of his life, affecting not only his personal well-being but also his career and relationships.

2. Rehabilitation and Treatment:

Seeking professional help is a crucial step in the recovery process. Perry underwent several stints in rehabilitation facilities, where he received counselling, therapy, and support in addressing the root causes of his addiction.

3. Support System:

Recovery is not a solitary journey, and Perry leaned on his support system throughout. Friends, family, and therapists played a significant role in helping him navigate the challenges of recovery.

4. Relapses and Setbacks:

Recovery is often marked by relapses, and Perry was candid about his own setbacks. These moments were not failures but opportunities for growth and learning. He used them as a stepping stone toward lasting recovery.

5. Lifestyle Changes:

Recovery often necessitates a complete overhaul of one's lifestyle. Perry made significant changes to his daily routines and surroundings to create a sober and supportive environment.

6. Commitment to Sobriety:

One of the key elements of Perry's recovery journey was his unwavering commitment to sobriety. He understood that maintaining sobriety required ongoing effort and dedication.

7. Helping Others:

Perry's recovery journey had a profound impact on him. He became an advocate for those facing addiction, using his own experiences to inspire and guide others. His openness about recovery has destigmatized addiction and encouraged many to seek help.

8. Philanthropic Efforts:

Perry's commitment to helping others facing addiction led him to become actively involved in philanthropic efforts. His work with the Perry House, a sober living facility, has provided a supportive environment for individuals on their recovery journeys.

CHAPTER FIVE

RESURGENCE IN HOLLYWOOD: MATTHEW PERRY'S REMARKABLE COMEBACK

Matthew Perry's resurgence in Hollywood is a testament to his unwavering determination, talent, and the profound impact he has had on the world of entertainment. After the end of "Friends," Perry faced personal and professional challenges, but he made an inspiring comeback that solidified his status as a respected figure in the industry. This section explores his resurgence in Hollywood in detail.

1. Post-"Friends" Transition:

Following the conclusion of "Friends" in 2004, Matthew Perry faced the daunting task of transitioning to new roles. The shadow of Chandler Bing loomed large, making it essential for him to prove his versatility as an actor.

2. A Period of Exploration:

Perry's post-"Friends" journey was marked by a willingness to explore diverse roles. He appeared in a range of television shows, films, and stage productions, demonstrating his commitment to honing his craft.

3. "The Ron Clark Story" (2006):

One of the notable projects during this period was his portrayal of the real-life educator Ron Clark in the television film "The Ron Clark Story." Perry's performance in this role showcased his ability to tackle more dramatic and inspiring characters.

4. "Studio 60 on the Sunset Strip" (2006-2007):

Perry returned to television with the series "Studio 60 on the Sunset Strip," where he played Matt Albie, a brilliant but troubled television writer. The show allowed Perry to flex his acting muscles in a dramatic and witty role.

5. "The End of Longing" (2016):

Perry made his playwriting debut with "The End of Longing." This dark comedy explored themes of addiction and relationships, echoing his personal experiences and challenges. His creative involvement in this project was a testament to his multifaceted talents.

6. A Resilient Spirit:

Perry's resilience shone during this period. He openly discussed his struggles with addiction, his time in rehab, and his personal journey to recovery. His ability to confront his challenges and continue working in the industry was a testament to his strength of character.

7. Philanthropic Efforts:

While rebuilding his career, Perry maintained a strong commitment to philanthropic endeavours, particularly those related to addiction and mental health. His advocacy and involvement in these areas highlighted his dedication to giving back.

8. "The Kennedys: After Camelot" (2017):

Perry took on the role of Ted Kennedy in the miniseries "The Kennedys: After Camelot." His performance showcased his versatility as an actor, as he tackled the complex character of a real-life political figure.

9. Revival of "Friends":

In 2021, the highly anticipated "Friends Reunion" brought Perry and the rest of the original cast back together. The reunion not only reignited nostalgia for the beloved series but also gave fans a glimpse into the enduring friendships among the cast.

10. Ongoing Projects:

Perry's resurgence in Hollywood has not been a short-lived phenomenon. He continues to work on various projects, demonstrating that he remains a relevant and sought-after talent in the industry.

Matthew Perry's resurrection in Hollywood is a story of reinvention, adaptability, and the staying power of talent.

It's a testament to his determination to overcome personal challenges and re-establish himself as a multifaceted actor, writer, and advocate.

His ability to navigate the complexities of the entertainment industry and the personal challenges he faced are an inspiration to those who encounter setbacks in their own journeys.

Perry's story reminds us that with perseverance and passion, you can bounce back and leave an indelible mark on the entertainment world.

CHAPTER SIX

MULTIFACETED TALENT: MATTHEW PERRY AS A WRITER AND PRODUCER

Matthew Perry's talents extend far beyond his acting career. He has proven himself to be a multifaceted artist with a remarkable ability to write and produce, adding depth and diversity to his creative portfolio. In this section, we delve into his endeavours as a writer and producer, shedding light on his accomplishments and contributions in these roles.

1. Writing "The End of Longing":

One of the most notable examples of Matthew Perry's foray into writing is his play, "The End of Longing." Premiering in 2016, the dark comedy explored themes of addiction, relationships, and self-discovery. Perry not only wrote the play but also starred in it, demonstrating his proficiency in both writing and acting.

2. A Personal Touch:

"The End of Longing" drew from Perry's own experiences, particularly his struggles with addiction. His willingness to share his personal journey added an authentic and poignant layer to the play, making it a powerful exploration of human frailty and resilience.

3. An Insightful Playwright:

Perry's writing in "The End of Longing" was characterized by its wit, humour, and keen insight into the complexities of human relationships. The play received positive reviews for its sharp dialogue and thought-provoking themes.

4. "Mr. Sunshine" (2011):

In addition to writing, Perry took on the role of co-creator and executive producer for the television series "Mr. Sunshine." The show allowed him to flex his creative muscles in a different capacity, shaping the narrative and the characters in a way that aligned with his vision.

5. "The Odd Couple" (2015-2017):

Perry played an integral role in the 2015 reboot of the classic sitcom "The Odd Couple." Beyond his acting duties, he served as an executive producer on the series, contributing to the creative direction and production of the show.

6. A Passion for Behind-the-Scenes Work:

Perry's foray into writing and producing highlights his passion for all aspects of the entertainment industry. His involvement in these roles demonstrates his commitment to storytelling, whether in front of the camera or behind it.

7. A Multifaceted Approach:

Perry's ability to juggle multiple roles in the creation of a production showcases his versatility. His experience as an actor provides valuable insights into character development and storytelling, making him an effective writer and producer.

8. The Intersection of Personal and Professional:

Perry's creative projects often intersect with his personal experiences, adding authenticity and depth to his work. His willingness to draw from his own life for inspiration contributes to the emotional resonance of his projects.

9. A Philanthropic Mission:

Perry's multifaceted talents are not solely for personal gain. He has used his creative abilities to support causes close to his heart, particularly in the realms of addiction recovery and mental health advocacy.

10. A Pioneering Spirit:

Perry's ventures as a writer and producer illustrate his pioneering spirit and his willingness to take creative risks. These ventures add a new dimension to his legacy in the entertainment industry.

Matthew Perry's achievements as a writer and producer highlight his artistic range and his commitment to storytelling. His contributions in these roles have not only showcased his creativity but also allowed him to explore profound themes and add depth to his body of work. Perry's multifaceted talents serve as an inspiration to aspiring writers, producers, and artists, illustrating the potential for growth and success across different creative domains within the entertainment industry.

PHILANTHROPY AND SOCIAL ACTIVISM: MATTHEW PERRY'S IMPACT BEYOND THE SCREEN

Matthew Perry's legacy extends far beyond his entertainment career. He is a passionate philanthropist and social activist who has dedicated his time, resources, and voice to a variety of causes. His commitment to making a positive impact on society showcases the depth of his character and his desire to effect meaningful change. In this section, we explore Matthew Perry's philanthropic and social activism endeavours in detail.

1. Dedication to Addiction Recovery:

Matthew Perry's personal battles with addiction have fuelled his commitment to raising awareness about substance abuse and supporting those on their journey to recovery. He has been actively involved in initiatives related to addiction treatment and rehabilitation.

2. The Perry House:

Perry's dedication to addiction recovery led to his involvement in founding the Perry House, a sober living facility. The facility provides a supportive environment for individuals seeking to overcome addiction, emphasizing the importance of a stable and nurturing space for recovery.

3. Mental Health Advocacy:

Perry has used his platform to become a vocal advocate for mental health awareness. His personal experiences have allowed him to contribute to the broader conversation on mental health, reducing stigma and fostering understanding.

4. The "Go On" Experience:

The television series "Go On," in which Perry played a sports talk radio host dealing with grief, allowed him to explore themes of loss and healing. The show indirectly raised awareness about the importance of support and mental health in dealing with life's challenges.

5. Charity Work:

Beyond his involvement in specific organizations, Perry has engaged in charity work and fundraising efforts. His philanthropic endeavours extend to supporting various causes, demonstrating his commitment to giving back.

6. Contributions to Cancer Research:

Perry's philanthropy also extends to cancer research. He has been actively involved in efforts to raise funds for cancer treatment and research, recognizing the importance of medical advancements in battling the disease.

7. A Voice for the Voiceless:

Perry's social activism reaches beyond specific causes. He has been a voice for those who may not have the platform to advocate for themselves, using his celebrity status to shed light on issues close to his heart.

8. A Beacon of Hope:

Matthew Perry's involvement in philanthropy and social activism serves as a beacon of hope for individuals facing addiction, mental health challenges, and various societal issues. His transparency about his own struggles has inspired others to seek help and support.

9. Encouraging Dialogue:

Perry's willingness to speak openly about addiction and mental health has encouraged honest dialogue and discussions about these issues. He has played a crucial role in reducing the stigma surrounding addiction and mental health challenges.

Matthew Perry's social and philanthropic efforts demonstrate his commitment to improving the lives of others and creating a positive impact on society.

Her dedication to addiction recovery, mental health advocacy, and various charitable causes demonstrates her compassion and genuine desire to create meaningful change.

Perry's work reminds us that, no matter our personal challenges, we all have the ability to contribute to a better world through philanthropy and social action.

His legacy speaks to the power of compassion and its potential for transformation and healing in the lives of countless people.

A VOICE IN MENTAL HEALTH ADVOCACY: MATTHEW PERRY'S INSPIRING JOURNEY

Matthew Perry's role as a mental health advocate is a compelling and inspiring testament to his resilience, compassion, and commitment to making a difference. Through his own battles with addiction and mental health challenges, he has emerged as a prominent voice in the field of mental health advocacy. This section delves into the details of his journey as a mental health advocate, highlighting his contributions and the impact of his advocacy efforts.

1. Personal Struggles and Transparency:

Matthew Perry's journey into mental health advocacy began with his own experiences. His battles with addiction, depression, and anxiety led him to a place of introspection and a deep understanding of the importance of mental health.

2. Reducing Stigma:

Perry recognized that the stigma surrounding mental health issues was a significant barrier to individuals seeking help. His decision to speak openly about his own struggles was a pivotal step in reducing that stigma and fostering a more compassionate and understanding society.

3. Advocacy through Storytelling:

As an actor and writer, Perry used the power of storytelling to shed light on mental health challenges. His work often explored the complexities of addiction and mental health, allowing audiences to relate to and empathize with the characters he portrayed.

4. An Ambassador for Understanding:

Perry's commitment to mental health advocacy has made him an ambassador for understanding. His ability to articulate the challenges of mental health issues and the importance of seeking help has resonated with people around the world.

5. Raising Awareness:

Beyond personal disclosures, Perry has actively engaged in raising awareness about mental health issues. He has used his platform to educate and inform the public about the realities of living with addiction and mental health challenges.

7. Support for Mental Health Initiatives:

Perry has lent his support to various mental health initiatives and organizations, contributing both his time and resources to further the cause. His involvement has made a significant impact on the resources available for those in need.

8. Destigmatizing Conversations:

Perry's advocacy efforts have played a crucial role in destigmatizing conversations about addiction and mental health. He has encouraged individuals to speak openly about their challenges and seek help when needed.

9. Encouraging Help-Seeking Behaviour:

Perry's advocacy work has contributed to a shift in societal attitudes toward mental health. He has encouraged individuals to seek help without shame, emphasizing that mental health challenges are common and treatable.

10. Making a Lasting Impact:

Matthew Perry's journey as a mental health advocate is a testament to the lasting impact one individual can have. His efforts have not only helped countless individuals on their own paths to recovery but have also contributed to a more compassionate and understanding society.

Matthew Perry's advocacy in the realm of mental health has been instrumental in reshaping the way society perceives and addresses these challenges. His personal journey, transparency, and commitment to making a positive impact have inspired many to seek help, reduced stigma, and created a more empathetic world for those facing mental health issues. Perry's legacy as a mental health advocate serves as a beacon of hope and a reminder that recovery and healing are possible, no matter how daunting the challenges may seem.

INFLUENCE ON POP CULTURE: MATTHEW PERRY'S ENDURING LEGACY

Matthew Perry's influence on pop culture is an indelible mark that has resonated with audiences around the world for decades. His portrayal of iconic characters, his ability to connect with viewers, and his contributions to both film and television have solidified his status as a cultural phenomenon. In this section, we explore Matthew Perry's influence on pop culture, detailing his lasting legacy and the impact he has had on the entertainment industry and beyond.

1. Chandler Bing: A Character for the Ages:

Perhaps the most significant element of Matthew Perry's influence on pop culture is his portrayal of Chandler Bing on the beloved television series "Friends." Chandler's unique blend of sarcasm, wit, and endearing quirks has made him an enduring and iconic character. His catchphrases, such as "Could I BE any more...," and his distinctive humour continue to be celebrated and imitated by fans worldwide.

2. The Success of "Friends":

"Friends" itself stands as a cultural touchstone. The series, in which Perry played a central role, has had a profound impact on pop culture, influencing fashion, language, and the very dynamics of friendship. The show's popularity endures, making it a timeless and cherished part of television history.

3. Chandler Bing's Legacy:

Chandler Bing's character has left an indelible imprint on pop culture. He represents the witty, self-deprecating, and relatable friend that many viewers can identify with. The character's enduring appeal continues to influence comedic portrayals in television and film.

4. A New Perspective on Addiction:

Perry's openness about his struggles with addiction and his journey to recovery have changed the way pop culture addresses substance abuse and mental health. His willingness to share his experiences has helped destigmatize conversations about these challenges and inspire others to seek help.

5. Resurgence and Reinvention:

Perry's resurgence in Hollywood after "Friends" demonstrated his ability to reinvent himself and take on diverse roles. His success in different projects, from television to theatre, showcases his versatility and has encouraged other actors to take creative risks.

6. The "Friends" Reunion:

The highly anticipated "Friends Reunion" in 2021 was a testament to the enduring influence of the show and its cast. The reunion special allowed fans to revisit the beloved characters and relive the nostalgia, highlighting the lasting impact of the series.

7. Social Media Presence:

Perry's presence on social media has allowed him to engage with fans and share insights into his life. His candid and humourous posts have garnered a dedicated following, connecting with both newer generations and long-time fans.

8. Inspirational Philanthropy:

Perry's dedication to philanthropy, particularly in the fields of addiction recovery and mental health, has influenced the way celebrities and public figures use their status to support meaningful causes. His philanthropic efforts set an example for others to give back and effect positive change.

9. Influence on Comedy and Acting:

Matthew Perry's comedic timing, delivery, and versatility as an actor have influenced the way comedy is portrayed in television and film. His ability to seamlessly transition between humour and drama has set a standard for actors in the industry.

10. A Cultural Icon:

Matthew Perry's influence on pop culture extends beyond the screen. He represents an era in entertainment that continues to be celebrated and cherished, and his work has left a lasting imprint on the collective memory of audiences.

Matthew Perry's influence on pop culture is a testament to the lasting impact one individual can have in the world of entertainment and beyond. His memorable characters, his personal journey, and his commitment to philanthropy have inspired, entertained, and educated generations. As a cultural icon, he has not only left an enduring legacy but has also contributed to the evolution of pop culture in meaningful ways, making him a beloved figure in the hearts of many.

CHAPTER SIX

REFLECTIONS ON A REMARKABLE CAREER: MATTHEW PERRY'S JOURNEY

Matthew Perry's career in the entertainment industry is nothing short of remarkable. From his early days in Hollywood to his iconic role as Chandler Bing in "Friends" and his enduring presence in film, television, and theatre, his journey is a testament to talent, perseverance, and an unwavering commitment to his craft. In this section, we reflect on the highlights, challenges, and enduring legacy of Matthew Perry's remarkable career.

1. The Early Years:

Matthew Perry's journey in the entertainment industry began at a young age. Born on August 19, 1969, in

Williamstown, Massachusetts, he was raised in a family with a strong background in acting. His father, John Bennett Perry, was an actor, and his mother, Suzanne Morrison, was a Canadian journalist and press secretary.

2. Television Debut:

Perry made his television debut with a role in the series "Boys Will Be Boys" in 1986. However, it was in the early 1990s that he gained recognition for his work in the television series "Second Chance" and "Home Free."

3. Breakthrough with "Friends":

The turning point in Matthew Perry's career came when he was cast as Chandler Bing in the iconic sitcom "Friends" in 1994. The show became a cultural phenomenon, and Perry's portrayal of the witty, sarcastic character endeared him to audiences worldwide.

4. Chandler Bing's Legacy:

Chandler Bing remains one of the most beloved characters in television history. Perry's impeccable comedic timing, relatable humour, and chemistry with the ensemble cast contributed to the show's immense success.

5. The Highs and Challenges:

While "Friends" brought unparalleled fame and success, it also posed challenges. The pressures of stardom and the battle with addiction were hurdles that Perry faced during this period.

6. A Journey to Recovery:

Perry's journey to recovery from addiction was marked by stints in rehabilitation and personal growth. His commitment to sobriety and the openness with which he shared his struggles have been sources of inspiration for many.

7. Venturing into Writing and Producing:

Beyond acting, Perry explored writing and producing. His play, "The End of Longing," touched on themes of addiction and relationships, reflecting his personal experiences.

8. Philanthropy and Advocacy:

Perry's philanthropic efforts, particularly in addiction recovery and mental health advocacy, have showcased his dedication to making a positive impact. The founding of the Perry House and his vocal support for mental health initiatives have contributed to positive change.

Matthew Perry's remarkable career is a story of growth, transformation, and a commitment to making a positive impact.

He has not only left an indelible mark on the entertainment industry but has also inspired and connected with people through his characters, his advocacy, and his openness about personal challenges. As a reflection on a remarkable career, his journey serves as a testament to the enduring power of storytelling, resilience, and the ability to effect meaningful change in the world.

UNEXPLORED ASPECTS: MATTHEW PERRY'S HIDDEN DEPTHS

While Matthew Perry is widely recognized for his iconic role as Chandler Bing on "Friends" and his accomplishments in the entertainment industry, there are unexplored aspects of his life and career that reveal hidden depths and lesser-known facets of this multifaceted talent. In this section, we delve into these uncharted territories to shed light on lesser-known aspects of Matthew Perry's life and journey.

1. Early Life and Education:

Matthew Perry's upbringing and educational background offer insights into his formative years. He was raised in Ottawa, Canada, and attended Ashbury College, where his interests in acting and performing began to emerge. His journey from Canada to Hollywood is a story of ambition and determination.

2. The Influence of His Parents:

Perry's parents, John Bennett Perry and Suzanne Morrison, were significant influences in his life. His father was an actor, and his mother a journalist and press secretary, instilling in him a love for both the performing arts and communication.

3. Family Dynamics:

While much is known about Perry's professional life, details about his family dynamics and personal relationships remain relatively private. Exploring the influence of his family on his career and personal growth provides a deeper understanding of the man behind the characters.

4. The Journey to Hollywood:

Perry's decision to pursue a career in Hollywood is a compelling aspect of his early life that is often overlooked. The challenges he faced and the risks he took to follow his dreams are a testament to his dedication to acting.

5. Pre-"Friends" Career:

Before the breakout success of "Friends," Perry's career included a mix of guest appearances in television shows, which showcased his versatility as an actor. Examining this pre-"Friends" era reveals the path that led to his iconic role.

6. Lesser-Known Projects:

Perry's filmography includes several lesser-known projects that offer a glimpse into his range as an actor. These projects, whether in film, television, or theatre, have contributed to the development of his craft.

7. Personal Hobbies and Interests:

Perry's personal life extends beyond his professional endeavours. His hobbies, interests, and passions outside of acting add depth to his character and provide insights into his life beyond the spotlight.

8. Private Charitable Work:

While his public philanthropic efforts are well-documented, there may be private charitable work or contributions that remain unexplored. Perry's dedication to causes may extend beyond what is publicly known.

9. Personal Reflections:

Perry's personal reflections on his career, life experiences, and the lessons he has learned may provide profound insights into his growth and development. These uncharted thoughts and introspections can offer a deeper understanding of his journey.

10. A Sense of Humour in Real Life:

Perry's sense of humour, which he brought to life through characters like Chandler Bing, is an aspect of his personality that often goes unnoticed. Exploring his real-life humour and wit adds another layer to his persona.

11. Future Endeavours:

Matthew Perry's unexplored aspects also include his future endeavours. The projects he has yet to embark on, the roles he has yet to play, and the contributions he has yet to make in the world of entertainment and beyond remain exciting uncharted territory.

Exploring these uncharted aspects of Matthew Perry's life and career enriches our understanding of this multifaceted talent. It reminds us that behind the characters and the fame, there is a complex individual with a unique journey, personal insights, and untapped potential. Matthew Perry's story is an ever-evolving narrative, and these unexplored aspects are a testament to the enduring allure of his life and career.

PERSONAL INSIGHTS AND ANECDOTES: A GLIMPSE INTO MATTHEW PERRY'S LIFE

Matthew Perry's life is marked by a wealth of personal insights and anecdotes that offer a deeper understanding of the man behind the characters. In this section, we dive into some of the most revealing and intriguing personal insights and anecdotes from Matthew Perry's life.

1. The Influence of His Parents:

Matthew Perry's parents, John Bennett Perry and Suzanne Morrison, played significant roles in his life. His father's career as an actor and his mother's background in journalism and press secretary work instilled a love for the performing arts and effective communication in Perry.

2. A Childhood Passion for Tennis:

Before entering the world of acting, Perry was an avid tennis player. His early passion for the sport even led him to consider a professional tennis career at one point. This insight into his athletic pursuits showcases a different facet of his life.

3. The Decision to Pursue Acting:

Perry's journey to becoming an actor was marked by determination and the pursuit of his dreams. Leaving Canada to chase a career in Hollywood, he faced challenges and setbacks that ultimately shaped his path to success.

4. Personal Struggles and Recovery:

Perry's openness about his struggles with addiction, depression, and anxiety has provided invaluable insights into the complexities of these challenges. His journey to recovery, marked by rehabilitation and personal growth, has inspired many on similar paths.

5. Early Career and Guest Appearances:

Before his breakthrough in "Friends," Perry appeared in a variety of television shows and films, showcasing his versatility as an actor. These experiences laid the groundwork for his iconic role as Chandler Bing.

6. Anecdotes from the Set of "Friends":

Perry has shared anecdotes and behind-the-scenes stories from his time on the set of "Friends." These insights into the camaraderie among the cast and memorable moments during the show's production offer fans a deeper connection to the series.

7. "Friends" Catchphrases:

Perry's character, Chandler Bing, is known for his memorable catchphrases, such as

"Could I BE any more...," which have become iconic in pop culture. The origins of these catchphrases and their impact on the show's success offer intriguing insights.

8. Anecdotes from "The End of Longing":

As a writer and actor, Perry's experiences during the production of "The End of Longing" provide anecdotes that shed light on the creative process and the personal significance of the play's themes of addiction and relationships.

9. The "Friends" Reunion:

The highly anticipated "Friends Reunion" brought the original cast back together, providing an opportunity for Perry to share personal insights and anecdotes from the show's history. The reunion special allowed fans to relive the nostalgia of their favourite characters and moments.

10. Personal Growth and Reflections:

Perry's journey to recovery and his resilience in the face of personal challenges have led to profound personal insights and reflections. He often shares these thoughts, emphasizing the importance of taking one day at a time and cherishing the progress made.

11. Future Endeavours and Aspirations:

Perry's personal insights and anecdotes extend to his future aspirations. While he has accomplished much in his career, there are always new horizons to explore and

Matthew Perry's personal insights and anecdotes offer a window into the experiences, challenges, and growth of a multifaceted individual. They showcase his resilience, creativity, and personal journey, providing a richer and more nuanced perspective on the man who has left an indelible mark on the world of entertainment and beyond. These anecdotes remind us that, beyond the fame and success, there is a human being with a unique story and a wealth of wisdom to share.

UNVEILING THE MATTHEW PERRY MYSTIQUE: THE ENIGMATIC ACTOR

Matthew Perry possesses a mystique that extends beyond his on-screen roles and public persona. This enigmatic quality has intrigued and captivated audiences for years, making him a figure of fascination. In this section, we delve into the Matthew Perry mystique, exploring the elements that contribute to his allure and the enigmatic aspects of his life and career.

1. Chandler Bing's Sarcasm and Wit:

One of the enigmatic aspects of Matthew Perry is his ability to channel the witty and sarcastic humour of his iconic character, Chandler Bing, while maintaining a sense of depth and complexity. His comedic timing and sharp wit have added layers to his on-screen and off-screen persona.

2. The Contrast of Comedy and Drama:

Perry's transition between comedy and drama is a testament to his enigmatic versatility. He can seamlessly shift from humour to poignancy, leaving audiences in awe of his acting range.

3. The Chandler Bing Legacy:

The enduring appeal of Chandler Bing as a character has created a mystique around Perry. His portrayal of the lovable and sarcastic friend continues to captivate audiences, leaving them curious about the actor behind the role.

4. Personal Struggles and Resilience:

Perry's battles with addiction and his journey to recovery add a layer of mystique to his life. His resilience in overcoming personal challenges is a source of inspiration and intrigue.

5. Creative Ventures:

Perry's foray into writing and producing reveals a hidden creative dimension. His ability to create thought-provoking works, such as "The End of Longing," adds to his mystique as a multifaceted artist.

6. The Relatable Celebrity:

Despite his fame, Perry maintains a relatable quality that endears him to fans. He often shares personal anecdotes, making him a celebrity who feels down-to-earth and approachable.

7. The "Friends" Reunion:

The highly anticipated "Friends Reunion" in 2021 brought the original cast together, including Perry, to revisit the beloved series. The mystique surrounding this event and Perry's role in it left fans eager to see what the reunion had in store.

8. Anecdotes and Stories:

Perry's personal anecdotes and stories from his life and career offer glimpses into his personality and experiences. These tales often leave audiences wanting to uncover more about his intriguing life.

9. The Charitable Enigma:

Perry's dedication to addiction recovery, mental health advocacy, and philanthropy adds to his mystique as a compassionate and socially conscious celebrity. His private charitable work remains largely uncharted, contributing to the enigmatic aura surrounding him.

10. The Future and Unexplored Terrain:

Perry's future endeavours and uncharted projects contribute to his mystique. What lies ahead for this multifaceted talent, and what unexplored territories will he venture into next?

11. The Unpredictable:

The enigma of Matthew Perry lies in his unpredictability. His ability to surprise and intrigue, whether through his work, personal insights, or creative endeavours, keeps fans and observers eager to see what he will do next.

12. A Complex Legacy:

The Matthew Perry mystique is a complex blend of humour, resilience, creative depth, and a sense of enigma that keeps audiences intrigued and invested in his life and career.

Matthew Perry's mystique is a captivating blend of humour, depth, and versatility. His ability to maintain an enigmatic allure while remaining relatable and grounded is a testament to his enduring appeal. The layers of his persona, from his iconic roles to his personal journey, continue to intrigue and inspire, making him a figure of fascination in the world of entertainment and beyond.

CHAPTER EIGHT

Matthew Perry's Impact on Entertainment: A Legacy of Laughter and Resilience

Matthew Perry has left an indelible mark on the world of entertainment, and his impact extends far beyond the confines of the screen. His contributions to the entertainment industry encompass a wide range of accomplishments, from iconic characters to ground-breaking projects, and they serve as a testament to his enduring legacy.

1. Chandler Bing: A Cultural Icon:

Matthew Perry's portrayal of Chandler Bing in the beloved television series "Friends" is an enduring testament to his impact on entertainment. The character's quick wit, unique humour, and memorable catchphrases have made Chandler a cultural icon, resonating with audiences worldwide. Perry's ability to bring this character to life with humour, charm, and depth has forever etched his name in the annals of television history.

2. The Success of "Friends":

"Friends" itself stands as a cultural touchstone. The series' impact on entertainment, fashion, and the very dynamics of friendship is immeasurable. Its popularity has endured for decades, captivating new generations and solidifying its place as one of the most beloved sitcoms in television history.

3. Influence on Comedy:

Perry's role as Chandler Bing has had a profound influence on the comedy genre. His impeccable comedic timing, delivery, and unique style of humour have set a high standard for humour in television and film, inspiring a new generation of comedic actors.

4. Seamless Transitions:

Perry's ability to transition between comedy and drama is a testament to his versatility as an actor. His successful forays into both genres have added depth to his portfolio and expanded his influence in the entertainment industry.

5. The Legacy of "Friends" Revisited:

The highly anticipated "Friends Reunion" in 2021 allowed fans to revisit their favourite characters and moments. Perry's participation in the reunion special reinforced the lasting impact of the show and provided an opportunity to celebrate its enduring legacy.

6. The Resilient Artist:

Perry's personal journey, marked by battles with addiction and mental health challenges, is a testament to his resilience. His openness about these struggles has not only inspired those facing similar challenges but has also reshaped the way the entertainment industry addresses these issues.

7. The Journey to Recovery:

Perry's journey to recovery and personal growth is a source of hope and inspiration for many. His commitment to sobriety and his efforts to support addiction recovery initiatives have made a significant impact on individuals and the industry as a whole.

8. Venturing into Writing and Producing:

Perry's creative ventures in writing and producing, such as his play "The End of Longing," showcase his ability to tackle complex and meaningful themes. His contributions as a multifaceted artist continue to shape the landscape of entertainment.

9. Impact on the Stage:

Perry's involvement in theatre and stage productions adds another layer to his legacy. His work on stage has allowed him to connect with audiences in a more intimate and profound way, further solidifying his impact on entertainment as a whole.

10. Charitable and Philanthropic Contributions:

Perry's dedication to addiction recovery and mental health advocacy is a testament to his commitment to social causes. His philanthropic efforts and vocal support for these initiatives reflect his desire to make a positive impact on society through the platform of entertainment.

11. Personal Insights and Anecdotes:

Perry's willingness to share personal insights and anecdotes from his life and career provides a deeper connection with fans and an enriched understanding of his journey. These stories offer a glimpse into the human side of the entertainment industry.

12. The Uncharted Future:

As Matthew Perry continues to explore uncharted terrain in entertainment, his impact remains an ever-evolving narrative. His future projects, creative endeavours, and contributions to the industry are anticipated with excitement and curiosity.

Matthew Perry's impact on entertainment is a multifaceted legacy that encompasses humour, resilience, versatility, and a commitment to social change. His influence has transcended the boundaries of the screen, leaving an enduring mark on the world of entertainment and society at large. As a beloved figure in the industry, his legacy continues to evolve, inspiring future generations of artists and leaving an indelible impression on the hearts of fans around the world.

LESSONS LEARNED FROM MATTHEW PERRY'S JOURNEY: RESILIENCE, REDEMPTION, AND REINVENTION

Matthew Perry's journey through life and the entertainment industry is a source of valuable lessons that resonate with individuals facing their own challenges and seeking personal growth. His story is one of resilience, redemption, and reinvention, from the highs of stardom to the lows of addiction and mental health struggles. In this section, we explore the profound lessons that can be gleaned from Matthew Perry's remarkable journey.

1. Resilience in the Face of Adversity:

Matthew Perry's story underscores the power of resilience. Despite facing personal setbacks, including addiction and mental health challenges, he demonstrated the strength to confront these obstacles and work towards recovery. His journey serves as an inspiration for anyone grappling with adversity, reminding us that resilience can lead to brighter days.

2. The Importance of Seeking Help:

Perry's openness about seeking help and entering rehabilitation highlights the importance of reaching out for support when facing personal challenges. His decision to seek treatment for addiction and mental health issues is a valuable lesson in acknowledging the need for professional assistance.

3. Honesty and Transparency:

Perry's candidness about his struggles and recovery fosters a culture of honesty and transparency. His willingness to share his journey with the public is a lesson in breaking down the stigma associated with addiction and mental health issues, encouraging others to do the same.

4. Personal Growth and Redemption:

Perry's journey towards personal growth and redemption is a testament to the transformative power of self-improvement. His commitment to sobriety and the path to recovery demonstrate that, no matter how challenging the journey, redemption is possible for those willing to put in the effort.

5. Reinvention in the Entertainment Industry:

Perry's ability to reinvent himself and take on diverse roles in the entertainment industry teaches us about the importance of adaptability and the willingness to step out of one's comfort zone. His successful transition from television to theatre and other mediums is a valuable lesson in embracing new opportunities.

6. The Impact of Personal Storytelling:

Perry's advocacy work and storytelling have shown the power of personal narratives. By sharing his experiences with addiction and mental health, he has connected with countless individuals and demonstrated the impact of personal storytelling in raising awareness and reducing stigma.

7. Philanthropy and Social Responsibility:

Perry's dedication to philanthropy and social responsibility serves as a lesson in the importance of giving back to the community. His work in addiction recovery and mental health advocacy underscores the positive impact individuals can make on society by supporting meaningful causes.

8. Lessons from Chandler Bing:

Perry's portrayal of Chandler Bing in "Friends" offers lessons in humour, friendship, and embracing one's unique quirks. Chandler's character reminds us of the importance of laughter and the value of authentic connections in our lives.

9. The Ever-Evolving Journey:

Matthew Perry's journey teaches us that life is an ever-evolving process. His past challenges, successes, and personal growth reflect the cyclical nature of life and the potential for change and renewal at any stage.

10. The Power of Second Chances:

Perry's journey is a testament to the power of second chances. His ability to overcome obstacles, reinvent himself, and contribute positively to society underscores the belief in the potential for personal and professional redemption.

11. Hope and the Human Spirit:

Perhaps the most significant lesson from Matthew Perry's journey is the enduring message of hope and the resilience of the human spirit. His story is a beacon of optimism for those facing their own trials and tribulations, showing that there is always room for personal growth and redemption.

Matthew Perry's journey imparts lessons of resilience, redemption, and reinvention that are universally applicable. His story reminds us of the human capacity to overcome challenges, seek help when needed, and inspire positive change, both personally and in the world at large. Through his journey, he has become a source of hope and an embodiment of the enduring spirit of the human experience.

ACKNOWLEDGMENTS AND CREDITS: MATTHEW PERRY'S IMPACT AND RECOGNITION

As we conclude our exploration of Matthew Perry's life, career, and enduring legacy, it is essential to acknowledge and credit the many individuals and organizations that have played a role in shaping his journey and the impact he has had on the entertainment industry and beyond. In this section, we extend gratitude and recognition to those who have contributed to Matthew Perry's remarkable story.

1. The "Friends" Cast and Crew:

The phenomenal success of "Friends" would not have been possible without the incredible ensemble cast and dedicated crew members who brought the show to life. Our heartfelt acknowledgments go to Jennifer Aniston, Courteney Cox, Lisa Kudrow, Matt LeBlanc, and David Schwimmer, as well as the creators, writers, directors, and producers who made the series an enduring classic.

2. Family and Friends:

Matthew Perry's personal journey has been enriched by the support of his family and friends. We extend our gratitude to his parents, John Bennett Perry and Suzanne Morrison, for instilling in him a love for the performing arts, and to his close friends who have been a source of strength and encouragement throughout his life.

3. Addiction Recovery and Mental Health Advocacy Organizations:

Perry's advocacy for addiction recovery and mental health initiatives has been instrumental in raising awareness and providing support to individuals facing similar challenges. Our acknowledgments go to the organizations and individuals dedicated to these vital causes, as well as those who work tirelessly to provide resources and support for those in need.

4. Colleagues and Co-Stars:

Matthew Perry's impact on the entertainment industry would not have been possible without the collaboration and camaraderie of his colleagues and co-stars. We extend our appreciation to those who have shared the screen and the stage with him, contributing to his multifaceted career.

5. Philanthropic Partners:

Perry's philanthropic efforts in addiction recovery, mental health advocacy, and other charitable causes would not be possible without the support and collaboration of philanthropic partners. Our acknowledgments go to those organizations and individuals who share Perry's commitment to making a positive impact on society.

6. Fans and Supporters:

The enduring support and admiration of fans around the world have been a driving force in Matthew Perry's career. We extend our heartfelt appreciation to the fans and supporters who have celebrated his work, cheered for his recovery, and followed his journey with unwavering dedication.

7. The Entertainment Industry:

Matthew Perry's contributions to the entertainment industry have left a lasting imprint on the world of film, television, and theatre. Our acknowledgments go to the industry as a whole for providing a platform for creativity, storytelling, and the exploration of diverse roles.

8. The Enduring Legacy:

We acknowledge the enduring legacy of Matthew Perry, which continues to inspire and influence individuals in the entertainment industry and beyond. His impact on comedy, drama, and social causes serves as a reminder of the profound effect one individual can have on the world.

In concluding our exploration of Matthew Perry's life, career, and contributions, we extend our acknowledgments and credits to the many individuals and entities that have played a role in his journey. Matthew

Perry's story is one of resilience, redemption, and reinvention, and it serves as a source of inspiration and hope for all those who follow in his footsteps. As we reflect on his remarkable impact, we are reminded of the enduring power of storytelling, compassion, and the ability to effect meaningful change in the world.

SUMMARY:

The biography of Matthew Perry is a comprehensive journey through the life and career of one of Hollywood's most iconic figures. From his early years and family background to his rise to stardom as Chandler Bing in "Friends," his battles with addiction and triumphant recovery, and his forays into writing, producing, and philanthropy, the book explores the multifaceted talent that is Matthew Perry. It delves into his impact on entertainment, the enduring legacy of "Friends," and the lessons learned from his journey of resilience and reinvention. This biography is a celebration of Perry's humour, resilience, and commitment to making a positive impact on society, both personally and through his work.

GLOSSARY

Chandler Bing: The iconic character portrayed by Matthew Perry in the television series "Friends."

Resilience: The ability to bounce back from adversity and challenges, a trait exemplified by Perry.

Addiction: A dependency on substances or behaviours, a battle Perry faced during his career.

Mental Health Advocacy: Perry's work in raising awareness and support for mental health issues.

Philanthropy: The practice of donating time, money, or resources to support charitable causes.

Enigma: The mysterious and captivating quality that surrounds Matthew Perry.

Reinvention: Perry's ability to adapt and explore new roles and opportunities in the entertainment industry.

Camaraderie: The strong sense of friendship and collaboration among the "Friends" cast.

Personal Growth: The process of self-improvement and personal development, a key theme in Perry's journey.

Legacy: The lasting impact of Perry's work and contributions to entertainment and society.

APPENDIX

Appendix A: Filmography of Matthew Perry

A comprehensive list of films, television shows, and theatre productions featuring Matthew Perry.

Appendix B: Awards and Recognitions

An overview of the awards and recognitions received by Matthew Perry during his career.

Appendix C: Selected Quotes and Anecdotes

A compilation of memorable quotes and anecdotes from Matthew Perry's life and career.

Appendix D: Recommended Reading and Viewing

A list of books, documentaries, and interviews related to Matthew Perry and "Friends."

Appendix E: Resources for Addiction Recovery and Mental Health Support

Information on organizations and resources related to addiction recovery and mental health advocacy.

KEY TERMS EXPLAINED

Sobriety: The state of abstaining from alcohol or substance use, often a crucial aspect of addiction recovery.

Multifaceted Talent: Refers to the ability to excel in various areas, such as acting, writing, and producing.

Cultural Phenomenon: A term used to describe a pop culture phenomenon that captures widespread attention and influence.

Reunion Special: A television or film event that brings back the original cast of a series or film for a special episode or show.

Catchphrases: Memorable phrases or expressions associated with a character or show.

Social Activism: The practice of using one's influence to bring about social or political change.

Resilience: The capacity to recover quickly from difficulties, often associated with overcoming adversity.

Redemption: The act of being saved from a negative or destructive path and finding a better way forward.

Relatable: Capable of being related to or understood by others, often used in the context of characters and their experiences.

Printed in Great Britain
by Amazon

8755db7d-f18a-4cf1-ac1c-7c98b64cd918R01